Christian Evidence Se

EVIDENCE FOR LIFE AFTER DEATH

by

David Winter

Published by Mowbray for
THE CHRISTIAN EVIDENCE SOCIETY

Copyright © David Winter, 1987
ISBN 0 264 67126 0

Reprinted with amendments 1989

First published 1987 for the Christian Evidence
Society by Mowbray, an imprint of Cassell, Artillery House,
Artillery Row, London, SW1P 1RT.

Typeset by Getset (BTS) Ltd., Eynsham, Oxford
Printed in Great Britain by Tisbury Printing Works Ltd., Salisbury

Evidence for Life after Death

ALL OF us die, about once in every seventy years or so. The strange thing is that we live as though we were immortal. Perhaps that explains why not only unbelievers but even Christians seldom discuss what sheer logic would tell us is the single most important question in the world: is there life beyond death?. Until recent times most people in the world believed that there was. Now many, at any rate in the once-Christian West, would either reply 'don't know' or 'probably not'.

Partly this is a response to a scientific rationalism which is now out of date for most intellectuals but still the predominant street and pub philosophy. Partly it is a reaction to an assumed obsession by our forefathers with the joys of the next world at the expense of pleasure in this. And partly it is the price the Church has had to pay for being half-hearted on this subject itself.

But St Paul, as so often, put the issue in perspective. If there is no resurrection, if 'our hope is only in this life', then we are, as he says, 'of all people most miserable'. Those whose horizons are limited to this material existence are like butterflies trapped in a larder. They are alive, but within confines. They move, but can never know what it is to reach the open sky.

The purpose of this booklet is to set out some of the evidence for life after death as a Christian sees it. It is largely based on and drawn from my book *Hereafter*, which has been around for fifteen years and been bought by over 200,000 people. It does not set out to *prove* life after death, because that is impossible. But it does set out to show that there is nothing intrinsically incredible, or even unlikely, about the idea that human personality survives death, nor even that we are raised as whole people – 'body, mind and spirit' as we say – after physical death in order to live on in another, better, God-centred existence: 'heaven', as Christians call it. And once we have opened our minds to the possibility, then perhaps faith can open reluctant eyes and stir up hidden hopes, leading us out of a rather arid

'this-worldly' obsession into the beauty of what the Bible calls
'eternal life'.

1. EVIDENCES FOR SURVIVAL

The evidence against survival is simply expressed: it is the evidence of our own eyes. When a person dies, they have 'gone'. However we express it, we regard their 'life' as ended. We talk about the 'departed' – or used to. Not only that, but we are familiar with death in so many other realms too. Plants, fish, and animals die, and in every case death is the 'end'. You may preserve their form but the life is gone.

In the nature of things, therefore, the evidence for survival is not so simply expressed. It has to overcome the apparently overwhelming evidence of our senses. And to introduce into it a concept which distinguishes between body and personality is to make the issue even more difficult.

Yet the fact is that the evidence is very strong. So strong that Dr John Beloff writing in *The Humanist* magazine in 1965 argued very persuasively that, rather than to try to deny 'survival', Humanists should accept that it probably occurs and look for a more 'rational' explanation than that offered by religion. He suggested a theory based on the electrical impulses of 'waves' produced by the human brain, which might continue functioning for some time – years perhaps – after death. But the point is that he felt it necessary to find a theory to explain a phenomenon which he accepted as more or less undeniable, and which might 'one day present a challenge to Humanism as profound in its own way as that which Darwinian Evolution did to Christianity a century ago'. The evidence for the paranormal points, he wrote, to a 'dualistic world where mind or spirit has an existence separate from the world of material things'. Humanists 'cannot afford to close our minds. . . to the possibility of some kind of survival whether in a discarnate or reincarnate form'.

What is this evidence for survival, and where does it come from? Those who suppose that it springs mainly from ghost stories and spiritualistic seances are rather out of date. The last century, and especially since the foundation of the Society for Psychical Research, has seen the amassing of an enormous amount of carefuly documented evidence on the subject. It does not follow that all of this evidence is equally relevant, and some of it may even be misleading, but it cannot be ignored. Contrary to popular opinion, the SPR is not concerned solely with so-called 'spiritualistic' phenomena; its members include people who are agnostic about survival, as well as some who are convinced supernaturalists. Its brief is to investigate in a scientific and controlled way any and all psychic manifestations, and over a period of years it has documented a vast amount of material relating to death and life after death.

Spiritualism and Other Paranormal Experiences

Let me say right away that very clearly a good deal of what is called 'spiritualism' is highly unspiritual. Much of it is fraudulent, or based on a combination of wishful thinking and hallucination. Let me also say that so far as I am concerned the practice of attempting to communicate with the dead through mediums is wrong and harmful, and is specifically forbidden in the Bible.[1] But, whatever the motivation and however undesirable the means, there undoubtedly exists a body of well-documented phenomena associated with 'spiritualism' which strongly suggests (to put it mildly) that human personality is not always extinguished at death.

Many years ago I met a young man who had recently become a Christian. Edward Atkinson had for twelve years previously been a convinced and active spiritualist, and one of the founders of the Young Spiritualist Council. His conversion was a painful and costly affair. He had frequently and publicly attacked Christianity, and on one fateful day, in his words, 'scornfully challenged the miserable carpenter who called himself God to invade, crush and re-make me'. And he did. In November 1961 Edward Atkinson left the spiritualist movement. But the faculty of clairvoyance only left him fifteen months later, and he was in the intervening period the subject of constant attack by spirits. Eventually, overcome by the reality of Christ in his life, they left him, and with them went his malign gift of clairvoyance. The significance of his story is this. Although he has spent much of his time subsequently warning Christians of the dangers of spiritualism, Edward Atkinson has never had any doubts at all about the reality of his earlier spiritualistic experiences or that he had in fact communicated with the discarnate spirits of the dead. [2]

The shadowy world of the 'spirits', from which discarnate 'voices' bring 'messages' to their loved ones on earth, is far removed from the heaven described by the Bible. I do not profess to know why some people after death seem able to communicate with living people through mediums, but I do not envy either them or the recipients of their messages. There is a better thing than this beyond the grave – but even saying that does not silence the testimony of these 'spirits' to the reality of 'survival'.

However, it is not the testimony of spiritualism that I am concerned with, except as an incidental factor. There are many well-documented accounts of experiences that testify to the survival of human personality beyond death.

A recent and very remarkable case is that of Edmund Wilbourne, a captain in the Church Army. His story was first made public on BBC Radio Merseyside in 1976, but it relates events that took place twenty-seven years earlier and were medically documented then. Captain Wilbourne's reluctance to publicize his astonishing experience is perhaps the most convincing argument for its authenticity.

He was critically ill in Crumpsall Hospital, near Manchester, with pleurisy and pneumonia. He died, and was in fact certified dead and his body 'laid out' by a nurse. At that point he seemed to leave his body, and could actually observe the nurse shaving and preparing his body for the mortuary. He felt linked to the body on the bed by a cord, but then the cord was severed and he arrived at a 'place' which he took to be heaven. It was, in his own words, 'nothing like floating on clouds or harps or anything of that sort', but a place of activity and meaning. 'I felt more alive and more alert than I've ever done since'.

Then he saw Jesus Christ, recognizing him by the print of the nails in his hands and his feet – as he thought at the time, they were 'the only man-made things in heaven'. He recognized other people, too, friends who had died, and was not at all pleased when an insistent voice grew louder and louder, praying 'O God don't let him die, he's got work to do for you'. Finally, as he explains, 'the Lord Jesus turned me round on my shoulder and gave me a gentle push, saying something to the effect, "It's not time for you yet"'. Captain Wilbourne came round, two hours after his 'death', in the hospital mortuary.

Subsequently, in an interview in a book,[3] he expanded on his experience of 'heaven'. He described it as a place of intense light and activity, with Jesus, light itself — and yet emphatically a 'person', in the same way as the other people he recognized: his Sunday school teacher, his mother and grandmother, and his doctor, who had died just previously. 'They did have physical shape', he recalls, 'but it somehow combined the youth and vigour of a twenty-one year old with a sense of perfect maturity.'

This account by Edmund Wilbourne has been parallelled in the experience of many others, though often less vividly. Certainly his description of a place of intense light beyond death is repeated over and over again in the accounts of people who have had similar experiences and so is this sense of separation of spirit from body at, or near, death.

I do not know how much weight one should attach to this kind of thing. It is not 'scientific' evidence, of course, as it is a non-verifiable record of an individual's private interior experience. However, when many sane and balanced people, over a long period of time but in roughly similar circumstances, record substantially the same experience, one must attach some weight to it.

A mountaineer has recorded a rather similar experience, not during the crisis of an illness, but during the few moments when he slipped over the edge of a precipice, hung some twenty feet over the edge on the end of a rope, and faced sudden death. His account is less documented, but just as interesting.[4]

I found myself hanging on the rope a few feet below the crest of the ridge. I turned, snatched at the rocks and clawed my way back. I had fallen altogether about twenty feet and the rope . . . had held . . . During the time I was doing this a curious rigidity or tension gripped my whole being, mental and physical. . . It was an overwhelming sensation and quite outside my experience. It was as though all life's forces were in process of undergoing some fundamental evolutionary change, the change called

5

death . . . I know now that death is not to be feared, it is a supreme experience, the climax, not the anticlimax of life.

'For how long I experienced this crescendo of power I cannot say, time no longer existed as time. . . Then suddenly this feeling was superseded by a feeling of complete indifference and detachment, detachment as to what was happening or likely to happen to that body. I seemed to stand aside from my body. It was not falling for the reason that I was not in a dimension where it was possible to fall. I, that is, my consciousness, was apart from my body and not in the least concerned with what was befalling it.'

Commenting on this experience, the author says, 'It is not within my province to discuss that which only death can prove; yet to me this experience was a convincing one, it convinced me that consciousness survives beyond the grave'.

Two further instances, both well documented and with all the marks of authenticity, seem to support that conclusion. The first is from the First World War, and concerns an apparition reported before the percipient knew of his friend's death.

The percipient was Lieut J.J. Larkin of the R.A.F. and the apparition was that of one of Lieut Larkin's fellow officers, Lieut David M'Connel, killed in an airplane crash on 7 December 1918. Lieut Larkin reported that he spent the afternoon of 7 December in his room at the barracks. He sat in front of the fire reading and writing and was wide awake all the time. At about 3.30pm he heard someone walking up the passage.

'The door opened with the usual noise and clatter which David always made: I heard his "Hello Boy!" and I turned half round in my chair and saw him standing in the doorway, half in and half out of the room holding the door knob in his hand. He was dressed in full flying clothes, but wearing his naval cap, there being nothing unusual in his appearance. . . I remarked "Hello! back already?". He replied, "Yes, got there all right, had a good trip". . . I was looking at him at the time he was speaking. He said, "Well, Cheerio!", closed the door noisily and went out.'

Shortly after this a friend dropped in to see Lieut Larkin and

Larkin told him that he had just seen and talked to Lieut M'Connel. (This friend sent a corroborative statement to the Society for Psychical Research.) Later on that day it was learned that Lieut M'Connel had been instantly killed in a flying accident which occurred at about 3.25pm. Mistaken identity seems to be ruled out, since the light was very good in the room where the apparition appeared. Moreover, there was no other man in the barracks at the time who in any way resembled Lieut M'Connel. It was also found that he was wearing his naval cap when he was killed, apparently an unusual circumstance. Agent and percipient had been 'Very good friends, though not intimate friends in the true sense of the word'. [5]

The second instance, the Chaffin Will Case, has become famous. As Rosalind Heywood remarks, 'Whatever the explanation, there is something to be explained'.

James Chaffin, a farmer in North Carolina, died in 1921 as the result of a fall, leaving a widow and two sons. In 1905 he made a will leaving his whole property to his third son, Marshall, who proved the will and himself died about a year later, leaving a widow and a son, a minor. In June 1925 the second son, James, began to have vivid dreams of his father appearing at his bedside and speaking. This vision may have been a 'borderland' experience, occurring between sleeping and waking. It was more realistic than pure dreams usually are but in an experience as informative as this the distinction is of little importance.

The figure was dressed in a black overcoat which James had often seen his father wearing. (James said that) 'He took hold of his overcoat this way and pulled it back and said "You will find my will in my overcoat pocket" and then disappeared'.

James went to his elder brother's house and found the coat, and inside the inner pocket, which was sewn up, a roll of paper with the words, 'Read the 27th chapter of Genesis in my daddy's old Bible'. James found the old Bible in a drawer in his mother's house and in the presence of witnesses found between two folded pages on which the 27th chapter of Genesis was printed another will, dated 16 January 1919, whereby the Testator, 'after reading the 27th Chapter of Genesis', in which the supplanting of Esau by Jacob is related, divided his property equally between his four sons, and added, 'You must all take care of your Mammy'.

The second will, though unattested by witnesses, was valid by the law of the state. . . Before probate, however, the Testator appeared again to his son, James, saying: 'Where is my old will?' and showing 'considerable temper'.[6]

These instances are cited in Rosalind Heywood's contribution to the symposium 'Man's Concern with Death'. She quotes the views of three distinguished scholars, none of them in any way committed to a 'survivalist' position.

First, the well-known American psychologist, Professor Gardner Murphy.

> 'Where then do I stand' To this the reply is: what happens when an irresistible force strikes an immovable object?. To me the evidence cannot be by-passed, nor, on the other hand, can conviction be achieved . . . Trained as a psychologist and now in my sixties, I do not actually anticipate finding myself in existence after physical death. If this is the answer the reader wants, he can have it. But if this means that in a serious philosophical argument I would plead the anti-survival case, the conclusion is erroneous. I linger because I cannot cross the stream. We need far more evidence; we need new perspectives; perhaps we need more courageous minds. (*Challenge of Psychical Research*, Harpers, New York 1961).

Next, the doyen of British psychologists, Professor Sir Cyril Burt.

> The uncertainty leaves the matter open in both directions. On the one hand the theoretical psychologist (and that includes the para-psychologist) should, on this particular issue, preserve a strict agnosticism, pressing physicalistic interpretations as far as they will go, and, even if in the end he feels compelled to adopt the hypothesis of a surviving mind, he must remember that it is, like the ether of old, no more than a hypothesis. On the other hand, those who, from reasons of faith, metaphysics, or what they take to be personal revelation, still wish to believe in survival for

themselves or those they love, need have no grounds for fearing scientific censure. Thus our verdict on the whole matter must be the same as that pronounced by Plato two thousand years ago – the reply he puts into the mouth of Socrates while waiting to drink the hemlock. 'I would not positively assert that I shall join the company of those good men who have already departed from this life; but I cherish a good hope'. Hope implies, not the virtual certainty of success but the possibility of success. And it is, I think, one important result of recent psychological and para-psychological investigations to have demonstrated, in the face of the confident denials of the materialists and the behaviourists, at least the possibility of survival in some form or other, though not necessarily in the form depicted by traditional piety or fourth century metaphysics. (In a symposium *Science & ESP*, Routledge and Kegan Paul.)

And finally, Professor C.D. Broad, sometime Knightbridge Professor of Moral Philosophy at Cambridge. He incidentally, does not hide the fact that he does not want to survive.

The position as I see it is this. In the known relevant normal and abnormal facts there is nothing to suggest and much to counter-suggest, the possibility of any kind of persistence of the psychical aspect of a human being after the death of his body. On the other hand, there are many quite well attested paranormal phenomena which strongly suggest the full-blown survival of a human personality. Most people manage to turn a blind eye to one or other of these two relevant sets of data, but it is part of the business of a professional philosopher to try to envisage steadily both of them together. The result is naturally a state of hesitation and scepticism (*in the correct as opposed to the popular sense of that word*[7]). I think I may say that for my part I should be slightly more annoyed than surprised if I should find myself in some sense persisting immediately after the death of my present body. One can only wait and see, or alternatively (which is no less likely) wait and not see. (*Lectures on Psychical Research*, Routledge and Kegan Paul, 1962).

The Resurrection of Jesus

However, none of these pieces of evidence, nor all of them taken together, is as full, as convincing, and as consistent as the best-documented 'survival' of all time, the resurrection of Jesus. Undoubtedly this must have extensive consideration in any book on this subject, whatever one's personal beliefs or convictions about Jesus Christ, if only because so much has been placed upon it and so much depends on it. It has been exhaustively studied, both by protagonists and antagonists, and is rightly reckoned to be the absolute lynch-pin of the Christian position on life after death. Even the apostle Paul saw it that way: 'If Christ has not been raised,' he wrote, 'your faith is futile and you are still in your sins'. [8]

On the other hand, the resurrection of Christ is not 'typical'. He claimed to be the Son of God. 'It was not possible for him to be held . . . by the pangs of death', the apostle Peter told the awe-struck crowds at Pentecost. [9] In his case, the body did not disintegrate, but was instantly transformed, leaving behind an empty tomb. This is not the path ordinary humans are called to walk; or rather, this is not the pace at which we are called to walk it. In the resurrection event – and the 'ascension', when the body of Jesus Christ returned to heaven – events which 'normally' take enormous periods of time are telescoped into a few days.

Yet in other ways it is entirely typical, and is clearly intended to be: 'In fact Christ has been raised from the dead, the first fruits of those who have fallen asleep'. [10] He is the beginning of a 'harvest' of resurrections, and in that sense is the pacemaker and the prototype.

So let us look at the resurrection of Christ, to see what it does, and what it does not say, about the more general question of life beyond death. There are several far more exhaustive treatments of the subject, and these are recommended to those who would wish to pursue the details and tie up all the ends. [11] In my treatment I shall restrict myself to the 'irreducible minimum' of what seems to me to be the heart of the matter.

Few people nowadays – and none at all who are taken seriously, I think – would deny that there was a man called Jesus who lived in Judaea in the early years of the first century

AD. His existence is not only attested by the Gospel writers (who might be considered prejudiced witnesses) but also by a number of distinguished secular or non-Christian historians – including the Roman Tacitus, and the Jew, Josephus. There is also an abundance of archaeological material showing how far and how fast Christianity – belief in this same Jesus as the Son of God – had spread by about AD 70. In other words, in a single life-time a man was born, lived, died, and became the founder of a major religion which held that he rose from the dead. This was not a peripheral belief about Jesus, something his followers could accept or reject as secondary. It was their message – 'Jesus and the resurrection'. [12]

Let us be absolutely clear what this means. Within the life-time of those who were eye-witnesses of the crucial events a major religion was born and spread with amazing rapidity which claimed that its founder, executed by the Roman authorities, had risen from the dead. No amount of argument over details about the crucifixion and burial of Christ can obscure this. They believed it – his contemporaries and his opponents, including the authorities who executed him, who were desperate to disprove the Christian case but were manifestly unable to do so. Unlike us, they had access to eyewitnesses. They could cross-examine them, and probe for flaws. Given the will to do so, it should not have been difficult to demolish so incredible an argument as that a man had risen from the dead. And the will existed, yet it was not done. One can only deduce that it simply could not be done.

It is sometimes said that those were gullible days, quite unlike our modern world; that people then were predisposed to believe all manner of weird and wonderful legends and fantasies. But this simply will not hold water. The first century was an age of cynicism and rationalism. The dominant Greek school of thought, Stoicism, did not believe in any kind of life after death. Neither did one of the two major Jewish theological groupings, the Sadducees. Thus there was no shortage of eloquent and learned voices to do battle against any religion or philosophy proposing as its central belief that a man rose from the dead. The reaction of the Greek Areopagus – a philosophical council – to Paul's message of resurrection is proof enough of that. They listened to him attentively until he spoke of Jesus being raised from the dead, but then the meeting broke up. This was the point of no return. Far from being gullibly disposed to accept it, they behaved exactly like their twentieth-century counterparts and mocked the very idea. [13]

So, from two assertions which are very nearly undeniable – that Jesus of Nazareth existed as an historical character in the first thirty or so years of the first century AD, and that by AD 70 the Christian religion was well established in the Graeco-Roman world – we are able to argue the strength of the case for the resurrection of Jesus. Those who care to refute it have got to face these facts head on, and find an explanation for them that is easier to believe than that Jesus rose from the dead. So far nobody has done it.

Of course, the 'case' for the resurrection of Jesus goes further than that. Any man who lives has to die, too. And it is historically consistent that he should have been 'crucified under Pontius Pilate' – the Roman Governor of Judaea at the time. Incidentally, we now have archaeological proof that Pilate actually existed – something earlier ages have lacked.

But on the third day after his death – the first 'Easter Sunday' – his disciples discovered his tomb to be empty. That empty tomb is an important piece of evidence.

After all, the burials of executed public agitators like Jesus are not hole-in-the-corner affairs. There had been talk earlier that he would 'rise from the dead', so obviously the authorities would take special care to see that he did not. We are told in the Gospels of a guard on the tomb, and of the sepulchre itself being sealed. But his disciples found that the tomb was empty, and within a few weeks were saying so publicly. Yet so far as history records, the authorities offered no counter to this remarkable claim. They did not produce the body of Jesus. They did not even produce the guards to say they had been attacked and the body stolen – though the idea was put up at one stage. The only recorded explanation offered by the anti-Christian parties was that this and all the miracles of Jesus were demonic in origin. [14]

But it was not just that the disciples found the tomb of Jesus empty. A number of them actually saw him, alive and vocal.

Later all the disciples saw him — indeed, according to Paul, more than five hundred saw him at once'[15] Not only that, but he adds 'most of whom are still alive'. That is the statement of a man confident of the truth of his evidence. Look, he says in effect, here is the proof that Jesus rose from the dead. He was seen at different times and places by all of the apostles, and then on one occasion by five hundred people . . . and if you don't believe me, you can check it for yourself, because most of them are still alive. As Paul wrote those words to the Church at Corinth, around AD 54, he was inviting sceptics to put his claim to the test. There were hundreds of eye-witnesses of the resurrection. True, they were a few hundred miles away in Judaea, but they were not inaccessible. Paul was presenting Christianity as it ought always to be presented — as an historical religion, rooted in certain events that actually happened at a place in geography and a point in history.

2. WHAT KIND OF NEW LIFE?

What was it that these Christian eye-witnesses of the resurrection saw? It is an important question, highly relevant to our investigation of life beyond death. It is not enough to say that they saw, or met, 'Jesus'. In what form did they see or meet him? Was he exactly the same in every way as before his death? If not, in what way had he changed?

Perhaps the simplest way to answer that is to draw up two lists, one of the dissimilarities between the pre- and post-resurrection Christs, and the other of the similarities.

Into the first list — the negative one — must go a number of pieces of eye-witness evidence which are frequently overlooked, or else seized upon to support a pre-conceived notion of the nature of Jesus after the resurrection. For example, it is really quite undeniable that the appearance of Jesus was changed, and changed to such an extent or in such a way that even his closest friends failed to recognize him. Mary of Magdala 'supposed he was the gardener'[1] on the morning of the resurrection. Two disciples walked seven miles to Emmaus with him the same day and did not recognize him until a familiar mannerism connected with giving thanks for the evening meal 'opened their eyes'.[2] Less obviously, Peter and the other disciples needed — and received – other evidence than the evidence of sight that it was in fact Jesus who met them during their fishing expedition on the Sea of Tiberias. This incident is in some ways the most revealing of them all. [3]

After the resurrection – and apparently slightly impatient at the delay in bringing in 'the kingdom' which they were expecting – seven of the disciples took a boat out on this inland sea for a night's fishing. But despite their professional skills, they caught absolutely nothing. However, 'just as day was breaking', Jesus stood on the beach and called to them. 'The disciples did not know that it was Jesus'. He told them to cast their net on the starboard side of the boat. They did, and caught an enormous quantity of fish. John then shouted to Peter 'It's the Lord!' and Peter, typically, leapt overboard and swam ashore to greet him. When the others followed, Jesus had lit a fire on the beach and they all had breakfast together. At this point John observes, 'Now none of the disciples dared ask him "who are you?" They knew it was the Lord'. Now obviously it was not the sense of sight that gave them this knowledge, or they would not have even thought of asking 'Who are you?' It was the miracle he had done, and the personality they knew so well, that convinced them that it was Christ they were meeting.

But it was not simply that the external appearance of Jesus was changed. The physical properties of his body were also changed, and very radically indeed. Although he specifically denied that he was a ghost or spirit[4] (and clearly he was not, because he could be touched, and he was able to prepare and eat a meal) and although he had 'flesh and bones', as the disciples could see,[5] yet he was able to enter rooms through locked doors,[6] appear in places many miles apart without apparently travelling by any recognized means, and eventually be 'taken from their sight' on the Mount of the Ascension.[7] It is hardly necessary to say that none of these things is feasible for a human body, and in fact none of these things happened to Jesus during his earthly life. Before the resurrection his body was unquestionably that of a normal human being. If he did not eat, he got hungry. If he did not drink, he was thirsty. At night he was tired and needed to sleep. If he was cut, he bled. The long journey from Galilee to Jerusalem took days, perhaps a week, and there was never the slightest suggestion that he might travel it in any but a completely 'normal' way.

Yet after the resurrection all this was changed. Quite obviously Paul was right when he claimed that 'Christ being raised from the dead, will never die again; death has no longer dominion over him'[8] That in itself says something very remarkable about the body of Jesus after his resurrection. All human bodies are mortal. They lie under the 'dominion' of death. Or, to put it in more usual language, they begin to die from the moment they are born. But this new body of Jesus was not subject either to the sudden onslaught of disease or accident, nor to the insidious and irresistible process of growing old.

And this body was not confined within the limits of our space-time world. It simply could not have been composed as 'ordinary' bodies are. It may indeed have had 'flesh and bones', but it was not limited by them in the way we are. Bars and bolts could not shut it out, and death itself could not touch it. It was a real body, there can be no doubt of that. Hundreds of people could not have been so mistaken, especially when Jesus offered clear evidence of it. But it was not an earth-bound body. It was something that bore a developmental relationship to an earthly human body, but it was not identical with it. There was clearly a continuity of life between the body of Jesus and the body of the resurrected Jesus, but in the process of resurrection it had undergone a very fundamental change. That, at least, seems obvious.

So much for the list of dissimilarities: the body of Jesus after the resurrection had a different appearance and also a different 'form'. It was 'like' the previous body, it had some sort of developmental relationship to it, but it was obviously not 'identical' with it.

Now we must consider the similarities. Strangely, they all came down to one factor, but that factor is so important that it outweighs all the dissimilarities. It is simply this: Jesus before and after the resurrection was undeniably the same person. No matter what extraordinary changes had taken place in his bodily form, all who knew him well had no doubt at all who he was. They 'knew' it was the Lord.

Let us see how they recognized him. Mary of Magdala

15

recognized his voice — or, possibly, a familiar mode of address: the way he said 'Mary'. The two on the road to Emmaus recognized his mannerisms: the way he broke bread. The disciples by the lake recognized his characteristic activity in the way he performed the miracle of the fish. More than that, of course, they recognized his characteristic thoughtfulness in lighting the fire and preparing breakfast. In other words they all recognized the person, or the personality, of a man they had known well, and were so sure it was him that they were prepared to die for that belief, as many of his early followers did.

What we arrive at, then, in examining the resurrection of Jesus is exactly what we found in all the other 'evidences' of survival: essentially what 'survived' death was his personality. But in this case an earlier supposition — that this surviving personality would need a new bodily vehicle in which to express itself — becomes a fact. The personality of Jesus after his resurrection from death expressed itself in a new body, no longer subject to limitations imposed on a spacetime, earthly body. The 'message' was the same — to use a favourite metaphor of Professor Donald Mackay — but the 'transmitter' was new and better, in general terms (less confined, less limited, immortal) and because it was specifically designed to live on in a spiritual environment, it was no longer really at home in this world.

The Transformation of Our Bodies

And this is the pattern, according to the Bible, for all resurrection. Not immediately at death, as in the case of Jesus, but just as instantly our bodies will be changed, and we shall enter a new environment in a form perfectly suited to life there. And it will be us: not our ghosts, not our 'souls', but the whole personality will break through the barrier of flesh and on into a new realm of living, just as it did with Jesus. The apostle Paul puts it very dramatically:

'Lo, I tell you a mystery. We shall not all sleep, but we shall all be changed, in a moment, in the twinkling of an eye, at the last trumpet. For the trumpet will sound, and the dead will be raised imperishable, and we shall be changed. For this perishable nature must put on the imperishable, and this mortal nature must put on immortality. . . . Then shall come to pass the saying that is written: 'Death is swallowed up in victory.'[9]

But what is the relationship between our earthly bodies and our changed heavenly ones? Is there any link, any connection at all? And if not, how can there be any 'recognition' of those we love in the life beyond death?

In a way, these questions have already been answered, if we accept the resurrection of Jesus as the prototype of all resurrection from death. As we have seen, there was a very real connection between the earthly body of Jesus and his risen one, but they were not identical. I have described the link as developmental, because that seemed a way of expressing the kind of unity which is involved. The second develops out of the first. It is a refinement of it, a further stage, a mutation, if we want a 'scientific' term. But it could never work the other way. The one is incomparably 'higher' and more advanced than the other. The continuity is of personality; the change involves the form in which that personality presents itself. Flesh and blood is our present form, with the limitations that that imposes. But what is to be our 'form' in the life beyond this earth?

The early Christians at Corinth put precisely that question to the apostle Paul. Here is his reply, in full.[10]

But perhaps someone will ask, 'How is the resurrection achieved? With what sort of body do the dead arrive?' Now that is a silly question! In your own experience you know that a seed does not germinate without itself 'dying'. When you sow a seed you do not sow the 'body' that will eventually be produced, but bare grain, of wheat, for example, or one of the other seeds. God gives the seed a 'body' according to his laws – a different 'body' to each kind of seed. . .

There are illustrations here of the raising of the dead. The body is 'sown' in corruption; it is raised beyond the reach of corruption. It is 'sown' in dishonour; it is raised in splendour. It is sown in weakness; it is raised in power. It is sown a natural body; it is raised a spiritual body. As there is a natural body so will there be a spiritual body.

It is written, moreover, that:

The first man Adam became a living soul.
So the last Adam is a life-giving Spirit. But we should notice

17

that the 'spiritual' does not come first: the order is 'natural' first and then 'spiritual'. The first man came out of the earth, a material creature. The second man came from heaven. For the life of this world men are made like the material man; but for the life that is to come they are made like the one from heaven. So that just as we have been made like the material pattern, so we shall be made like the heavenly pattern. For I assure you, my brothers, it is utterly impossible for flesh and blood to possess the kingdom of God. The transitory could never possess the everlasting.

Listen, and I will tell you a secret. We shall not all die, but suddenly, in the twinkling of an eye, every one of us will be changed as the last trumpet sounds! For the trumpet will sound and the dead shall be raised beyond the reach of corruption, and we shall be changed. For this perishable nature of ours must be wrapped in imperishability. . .

This statement repays close study, because in it Paul expresses the heart of the Christian (as compared to the pagan) doctrine of immortality. Here is no crude idea of dead bodies rising from their graves or miraculously re-assembling after cremation, but a profound picture of development from a simpler to a more complex form of life. Paul is quite clear that our earthly bodies die. They are 'perishable', with all that that implies. Those who ridicule the whole idea of resurrection must accept in fairness that Christianity has never taught that a dead human body is anything other than 'perishable'. If they wish to attack the doctrine, let them at least pay it the minimum compliment of getting it right first. Bodies die and disintegrate, and that is that, so far as the body is concerned. 'What you sow does not come to life unless it dies', says Paul, describing what happens when a seed is planted. When the plant has fully grown, what has become of the seed itself? It has gone, disappeared – its 'life' now part of a greater, more complex being, its 'body' utterly disintegrated. And that, he argues, is what happens to our bodies at death.

He goes further. There is to be a change of kind. For that he uses two analogies. The first is of different kinds of 'flesh' – earthly bodies. 'Not all flesh is alike,' he argues. 'There is one kind for men, another for animals, another for birds and another for fish'. [11]

In fact, of course, he is using unscientific language. In the strictly biological sense there is very little, if any, difference between one flesh and another. Flesh, after all, is flesh. But of course Paul was not using the word in the biological sense. 'Flesh' in the Bible is either the lower side of human nature or – as here – simply the bodily form of an earthly creature. There is a difference between the forms of men, animals, birds, and fish, but it is a difference within limits. They have life in common, and much else: senses, appetites, animation. But within a circle of comparability they are yet distinctively different. So – he clearly implies – is life after death from life before death.

Spiritual Life is Better

His second analogy is a rather obscure one to modern eyes. 'There are celestial bodies and there are terrestrial bodies; but the glory of the celestial is one, and the glory of the terrestrial is another. There is one glory of the sun, and another glory of the moon, and another glory of the stars, for star differs from star in glory. [12] It is tempting to read into it more than it can bear. All Paul is saying, it seems to me, is that once again within the created order there are differences within circles of comparability. Obviously the moon is different from the sun, and the sun is from the earth, and one star from another. But they are all bodies in space, 'heavenly bodies'. It is also very probable that, using the cosmology of his day, which saw the stars and planets in a sort of hierarchical order, he was also saying that within this limited similarity there was an ascending order of 'glory' from the lowest to the mightiest.

All of this leads on to his positive statement that spiritual (that is to say, heavenly) life is 'like' physical (that is to say, earthly) human life, but is more 'glorious'. Earthly life is perishable, crude, weak; heavenly life is imperishable, glorious, powerful. Yet there is a circle of comparability. They are not really two different things, but one is an extension or development of the other. 'But it is not the spiritual which is first but the physical, and then the spiritual.' [13] The development is not from a higher form of life to a lower one, but the opposite. There is, as we saw in the case of the risen body of Jesus, a developmental relationship between the earthly body and the resurrection body, but it is a development upwards. At death we move to a higher, not a lower plane of existence.

Now that is very important, if only because some 'survival' theories, including reincarnation and many kinds of spiritualism, imply the contrary. The wispy spirits who blow trumpets and tap out pathetic messages from the beyond could never be described, surely, as 'more glorious' than living, breathing, rational, earthly human beings? 'Glory' is simply not a word one could apply to most of them or their misty world of half-reality. Equally a man re-incarnated as an animal or an insect – or even another man – could not be said to have moved upwards to a higher, more glorious mode of existence.

The Resurrection Body

So the body we are to have after death (the resurrection body) is a development, a refinement of our present one, which disintegrates at death. There is a relationship between them, but the spiritual body is infinitely 'higher' and in every respect superior. The personality – the 'message' – remains, but the transmitter is a much better one.

The fact is that 'flesh and blood cannot inherit the kingdom of God'.[14] They are excellent vehicles for the message of the human personality in space and time, but quite inadequate for it in a mode of existence where space and time are meaningless concepts. That is why this great 'change' that Paul speaks of, this metamorphosis, has to take place. Just as the caterpillar has to be changed into the butterfly in order to 'inherit' the air, so we have to be changed in order to inherit 'heaven'. There is simply no alternative.

So let us stress again the most important fact involved here – that the spiritual body and the spiritual life are better, more glorious, more real than their physical predecessors. Once we have really got this into our thinking our whole attitude to death will be transformed. If all we have to look forward to at death is at best extinction, and at worst a shadowy ghost-existence in some twilight spirit world, then no wonder men and women face it with distaste and even fear. We do not enjoy the thought of ceasing to exist, but neither does a normal, life-loving human relish relegation to a kind of sub-life, which is all that non-Christian theories of 'survival' really amount to. The best of them do, it is true, look on to some kind of blissful union with 'the ultimate', but none, it seems to me, can match the Christian emphasis on the superiority at every level and in every way of the life that begins at death. This is the great theme of the fifteenth chapter of Paul's first epistle to the Corinthians: the 'resurrection' life is a life of power, achievement, splendour, beauty. It has everything good from this earthly life, but without the things that make it earth-bound, limited and frustrating. Over everything on earth hangs the dark shadow of time. We never seem to have enough of it to do all the things we should like to do, to become the people we ought to be or to get to know others as we should like to know them. And there are other limitations: pain, failing sight and hearing, physical handicaps and so on. All of these detract from the quality and satisfaction of life on earth, though in overcoming them men and women have achieved nobility and greatness.

Essential Humanity Survives

But in the life beyond death all of these are no more. 'God himself will be with them', says John in Revelation; 'He will wipe away every tear from their eyes, and death shall be no more, neither shall there be mourning nor crying nor pain any more, for the former things have passed away'. [15] Yet in losing them, we do not lose what is essentially human. We do not become ghosts. We carry over all that is essential (the 'kernel' as Paul put it [16]), but 'God gives it a body as he has chosen'. [17]

All of which emphasises the fact that if the Christian doctrine of resurrection is true – and I have tried to show how strong and consistent it is – then there is no need for distaste or trepidation in the face of death. All that lies beyond, for those who are to be raised in Christ, is superbly good. The God who made this earth so splendid, with its wonderful variety of colour and form, its joys of human love, family, and work and its magnificence of art, music, and literature, has himself promised that the next life will be better. What more could any doubter ask than that?

NOTES

(Section 1)

1 e.g. Leviticus 19.31; Deuteronomy 18.11.
2 His story was related by himself in *Crusade*, September 1964.
3 *Invitation to Healing* by Roy Lawrence, Kingsway.
4 F. S. Smythe. *The Spirit of the Hills*, Hodder, 1935.
5 Summarised by Professor Gardner Murphy in *Three Papers on the Survival Problem*, American Society for Physical Research, 1945.
6 W. H. Salter, *Zoar, or The Evidence of Psychical Research concerning Survival*, Sidgwick and Jackson, 1961.
7 My italics.
8 1 Corinthians 15.17.
9 Acts 2.24.
10 1 Corinthians 15.20.
11 e.g. *The Evidence for the Resurrection* by J. N. D. Anderson, IVP.
12 Acts 17.18.
13 Acts 17.30-32.
14 See *Beyond the Gospel*, R. Dunkerley, Penguin.
15 1 Corinthians 15.6.

(Section 2)

1 John: 20.15.
2 Luke 24.30-31.
3 John 21.1-12.
4 Luke 24.38-39.
5 Luke 24.39-43.
6 John 20.19.
7 Luke 1.9.
8 Romans 6.9.
9 1 Corinthians 15.51-54.
10 1 Corinthians 15.35-53 (J. B. Phillips' translation).
11 1 Corinthians 15.39.
12 1 Corinthians 15.40-41.
13 1 Corinthians 15.46.
14 1 Corinthians 15.50.
15 Revelation 21.3-4.
16 1 Corinthians 15.37.
17 1 Corinthians 15.38.

22